Moral Theories and Applications in Business:
An Introduction

Laurence Rohrer
Copyright© 2010 Laurence Rohrer

Published and Distributed by
The Educational Publisher
www.EduPublisher.com
ISBN: 1-934849-59-6
ISBN13: 978-1-934849-59-0

PREFACE

My overarching goal in this text is to provide a clear, concise, and comprehensible introduction to moral theory for students with limited or no background in philosophy. The idea for this text developed from my experiments using numerous sources for teaching business ethics since 1996. Over these years, I have struggled to find a text that offered the perfect balance of primary philosophical sources, business specific analysis, and useful case studies. Many of the comprehensive textbooks offered too little in the way of introducing moral theories, and often with no selections of the philosophers themselves. Others offer good coverage and discussion of many current issues but little in the way of in depth analysis. In this text, rather than create a single textbook that can do it all, I strive instead to introduce in some detail several of the most influential of the moral theories, and to critically clarify their scope and limits using a single recurring case study. The strategy is to demonstrate how our moral judgments change, and are differently informed by different moral theories. Each chapter offers a brief introduction and critical discussion of a different ethical approach. Excerpts of the philosophers whose works are seminal are included in each chapter. Thus, this book is not designed to be a stand-alone source for business ethics courses. It is meant to compliment other works, especially texts offering a good range of case studies, or perhaps a series of articles on contemporary debates in business ethics.

ACKNOWLEGEMENTS

I would like to recognize many people who were instrumental in the completion of this book. First, I am greatly indebted to all of the students I have been privileged to work with over the years, and especially to my recent students at Lincoln University, whose comments on the initial drafts of the materials used in this book were invaluable. This book is written for them. Second, I would like to thank my colleagues in philosophy at Lincoln University, Dr. Bruce Ballard and Dr. Jeff Freelin, for the many fruitful conversations about moral theories, and for their moral support. Finally, I would like to thank my wife, Barbara for her impeccable editing skills, and for reviewing every draft of this work, and for her many good suggestions on the style and structure of my chapters. Her patience and support never fails to amaze me.

Laurence Rohrer
Lincoln University, 2010

CONTENTS

CHAPTER ONE: ETHICS AND BUSINESS

1.1 The pursuit of moral truth

Ethics is the philosophical study of moral value. It involves several types of related questions. What is of highest value? What is virtue? What are the right rules of conduct? Are there objective moral rules? Are there absolute moral rules? With a little reflection, it is easy to see that while professional philosophers are interested in seeking the truth about these questions for its own sake these questions have everyday practical importance for non-philosophers as well. Not only should it be clear that each of us has a stake in the moral norms of our society, which define what is acceptable and inform our laws, but also we each have our own moral perspectives about controversial issues which we take to be true. When, for example, an anti-abortion proponent argues that abortion is morally wrong she is not understanding herself to be saying, "I am against abortion, but that's just my opinion. If it is ok with another person, that's fine." Instead, she means that abortion is wrong; therefore, people should not have them. Therefore, no matter how we answer the more overarching questions about the basis of moral value, and whether or not we will come up with answers that every person would accept, it is clear that most people do live their lives assuming that there are answers, and that these answers are objectively true. In other words, we take our moral beliefs to be true not only for ourselves, but for everyone else as well.

This observation often elicits the following response. Why do philosophers continue examining these questions, if in practical terms, we all behave as if we had the answers? There are several important reasons. First, as Socrates is portrayed as arguing in Plato's *Apology*, "the unexamined life is not worth living."[1] What is the point of a life in which we do not ever question our actions? How can we hope to improve our lot in life if we never examine our decisions and the assumptions on which they are based? Second, if we never examine moral issues, then we are apparently left with accepting whatever the status quo takes to be true. And we likewise must unthinkingly accept whatever legal decisions our community exacts. This can never be a good practice for any society, especially a democracy. A good example of the negative consequences of moral complacency and lack of ethical concern economically is clear from the scandal of the Enron Corporation in which countless shareholders were bankrupted due to the accounting practices of top CEOs. Likewise, the connection between the recent fall of the housing market and its drastic economic consequences is another case that points to the need for greater ethical and legal concern about market practices. Clearly there are moral issues about which our community disagrees. But can everyone be right? Just as clearly, there have been unethical laws, laws that have been repealed because they were considered immoral. Can we assume that all of our current laws are good ones and no further questions about their moral justification need to be asked? A complacent attitude of this type would make a society very ripe for the taking, easy to control, and susceptible to economic exploitation and political abuses. Finally, it must be recognized that a successful and humane democratic society must have not only informed citizens, but citizens who can comprehend political realities, and elect leaders who can critically and accurately examine moral and legal conflicts since the wellbeing of our society depends on such leadership.

All of this may seem trivially true. Nonetheless, we often hear people say "no one cares about ethics," or "there are no answers to these questions anyway, so why study ethics?" A good response to this attitude may simply be to remind these people, that if their houses were ever robbed, they should expect to be ignored. Why should society care about them, if they care about no one else? If they were robbed, they would most certainly complain and demand justice, and this would commit them to an inconsistency. At that point we could confidently say that they actually care about ethics after all.   In most cases, expressions about the irrelevance of ethics are not in fact said in complete earnest. They are merely a mark of complacency and intellectual laziness.   The pursuit of moral truth concerns us all. It is not solely an academic pursuit for a few specialists.

1.2 Normative and Meta-ethical issues

The study of **ethics** is commonly divided into two areas. **Meta-ethics** is concerned with questions about the meaning of moral statements, about whether or not there are objective standards for the use of such language, and whether such standards themselves are relative or absolute. In other words, meta-ethics raises questions about what we believe about the way we use moral language, rather than questions about whether a particular type of behavior is in fact right or wrong. **Normative ethics**, however, is concerned with questions of right and wrong and with developing standards and theories to apply to real life situations in order to make ethical decisions. Thus, in the first case, the statement, "all moral beliefs are culturally relative" would be a meta-ethical claim, a claim about all moral standards, not particular actions. In the second case, consider the example of the anti-abortionist mentioned in the previous section.   When she says "abortion is wrong," she is not making a meta-ethical claim, but rather a normative claim.   She is saying that the act of abortion is morally unacceptable, and should not be performed.   In other words, she is saying something that would imply that people should change their actual conduct.

The reader should note that there is a technical difference between the two terms "ethics" and "morals."   *Ethics* is the study of moral standards, and *morals* refer to the actual beliefs and standards of right and wrong that people hold.   However, for the purposes of this text, we will use the convention based on common usage and the two terms will be used interchangeably.

1.3 Business Ethics: Using Case Studies and Moral Theories

Business ethics is a topic area of normative ethics.   The use of the term "business ethics" should not be taken to suggest that businesses or business in general is subject to a special code of conduct.   Rather, we should recognize that among members of all organizations, and between all organizations in society, including businesses, there are moral issues, and these often result in legal conflicts.   In business ethics we study these issues and consider strategies to make responsible decisions about how business should be conducted in order to be ethical and in order to avoid litigation.

Ethical issues confronting businesses involve different **stakeholders**.   Stakeholders are persons or organizations that have stake in the practices of a business.   Some issues are **internal issues**, that is, issues that concern primarily members of the same businesses and their

4

shareholders. These issues often involve matters that must be resolved between employers and employees, and it typically falls to managers to deal with these matters. In contrast, the moral issues that exist between different organizations, in which the stakeholders are different companies, perhaps competitors, or between a business and a community, we will term **external issues**. While there are some issues that seem to fit both categories, this distinction is a useful one. It is important when studying ethical issues to take note of who the decision-makers must be, and these categories help us to clarify which stakeholders ought to be considered in making decisions and in suggesting ethical courses of action.

A related distinction in business ethics is often made between *domestic issues* and *global issues*. Domestic issues are those of national interest. For example, when a major U.S auto company lets go of part of its work force, this clearly has an impact on many stakeholders and the national economy as a whole. Global issues are involved when the stakeholders are different nations and the world economy. However, this distinction can be overstretched. Clearly, we now operate in a global economy. It has been well established that very few decisions that large corporations make fail to have profound effects throughout the world. This has led many to ask whether there are truly any purely domestic issues left when it comes to major companies. Likewise, it need hardly be pointed out that global economics affects all businesses, small ones as well as major corporations.

A common approach to learning to address moral issues is by evaluating **moral case studies**. A case study is simply a narrative that presents an event or series of related events involving ethical issues. Case studies present facts about the situation, the stakeholders, their roles and relationships, and, sometimes, legal allegations and actions that may be involved. Many case studies are based on actual historical events, such as the Enron scandal, and landmark cases such as the Exxon Valdez disaster.[2] Some case studies are fictitious, but present realistic situations in which present challenging questions. Case studies are useful because they present us with real-life events, but unlike many media stories, they provide us with enough facts to exercise our moral reasoning, and further speculate on how the moral issues might have been different if the facts had been different. It is important to learn to recognize situations in which we are confronted with a moral problem, and to learn how to make good decisions. In this respect, evaluating case studies helps develop moral discernment, as well as good reasoning.

There are two basic types of moral standards: **religious** and **secular**. A religious code of ethics is one that is based in a particular religious tradition. It may be based on a specific sacred text, such as the Bible, Koran, or the Hindu Vedas. In contrast, secular approaches attempt to answer moral concerns by an appeal to human reason alone, without reference to any particular religious assumptions or appeal to revealed truths. However, philosophers commonly refer to all types of institutionalized moral standards as moral theories. This habit can lead to a good deal of misunderstanding, so some clarification is needed. By theory, we often mean a secular theory. However, religious views would be excluded by such a use of the term. In this text we will understand the term **moral theory** in a more extended sense to mean any systematic attempt to account for morality that provides a basic claim about what is of highest value, and a set of principles that are purported to promote this value by guiding our actions accordingly. With this definition, religious perspectives are included as one type of moral theory.[3] While it is obvious that people's religious views often inform their moral beliefs, this text will focus primarily on philosophical moral theories that have often been embraced by both religious and non-religious people, and that inform current literature in business ethics.

Moral theories are developed by philosophers in order to try to capture the best standards for making rational moral decisions. All moral theories share some general characteristics, but differ in other ways. Here we will look at some of the common features of the theories covered in this book. We will explore their differences in the chapters that follow as we examine each theory in detail.

All moral theories make claims about human value. Using the classical approach, we can think of such claims as assumptions about the *highest good*, commonly referred to as the **summum bonum** by classical philosophers. In addition, every moral theory offers rules or principles that are intended to guide our actions. The concept is that if we follow these guidelines, we will be aiming at what is of highest value or doing what is morally correct. The authors of moral theories commonly offer examples to illustrate how the rules or principles should be applied in our lives. Similarly, religious texts offer stories in which exemplary individuals are portrayed exhibiting the right choices and best actions. For example, consider the story of Job, in the biblical Old Testament, or the portrayal of Jesus in the New Testament of the Bible. Secular moral philosophers also offer examples to illustrate how their theories are to be applied. They provide scenarios of real or fictional cases and discuss how their theories help resolve moral dilemmas presented in them.

Given that in this text we will be focusing primarily on secular, philosophical moral theories, we need to be aware of what philosophers consider to be the minimum features of good moral theories. First, a moral theory should be **rational**, meaning that it offers logical arguments to support its claims about the highest good and reasonable principles to guide our actions. This means that moral theories must also be **coherent**. The rules and principles of the theory should be consistent with one another and we should be able to consistently apply them to real-life situations. Second, many philosophers believe that a good moral theory must have **practical merit**, meaning that the theory must offer us insight into how to deal with difficult cases, not simply more clear cut ones. Third, most philosophers agree that our moral judgments ought to be as **impartial** as possible.[4] This means that moral rules apply to everyone, and in some theories, to everyone equally. For example, it would be unreasonable for someone to be angry with someone who rudely cut in front of him on the freeway, if he habitually does this to others. In this case, his judgment of this action would not be impartial, since he is exempting himself from a rule that he expects others to follow. Whether moral rules apply equally to all persons all the time is a controversial topic that we will explore in greater depth in the chapters ahead. As we examine each of the theories included in this book, we should compare and contrast them and consider their positive and negative aspects based on how well they satisfy these expectations of rationality, practical merit, and impartiality.

1.4 Two Problematic Views about Ethics

This section will address two common points of view about what we are doing when we make judgments about right and wrong: subjectivism and moral relativism. **Moral subjectivism** claims that all moral judgments are simply expressions of individual approval and disapproval. This implies that there is no objective standard that applies to everyone. **Moral relativism** claims that morality is relative to individuals, groups or cultures. In this book we will examine the most prevalent form of relativism, **conventionalism**, which states that moral standards are merely social conventions, and no one group's conventions are better or worse than those of another group. While both subjectivism and conventionalism are common, there are sound philosophical reasons for rejecting them.

Subjectivism can be summed up in the following way. Let us suppose that someone says "I believe that murder is morally wrong." What does this mean? The subjectivist is suggesting that all that this means is that the speaker disapproves of the act that is labeled murder. Likewise, if I say that I like to murder people and that I think that murder is not wrong, the subjectivist takes this to mean that I approve of murder. The subjectivist claims that there is no objective "right" or "wrong" regarding acts of murder or any other acts. Given this view, moral judgments are reduced to beliefs that are analogous to expressions of personal taste, such as differing choices about clothing or coffee. What are the reasons supporting this view? First, subjectivism cannot be logically disproved. However, this alone does not provide sufficient reason for accepting it. Moreover, what would count as evidence that it is correct? Perhaps the subjectivist might argue that people often disagree about moral matters. While this is true, the subjectivist fails to appreciate two facts about moral disagreements. First, rational people do not merely assert their moral views in such disputes, they argue for them, giving reasons to support their views. If subjectivism were true, there would be no need to offer reasons at all since every moral judgment would be a matter of personal preference. However, if every moral judgment is equal in this sense, wouldn't every action committed based on those judgments be equal, none better or worse than any other, in the grand scheme of things? Moral debate would be pointless. This would raise the question of how the same action could be both right and wrong. Second, we should ask whether or not subjectivism is a practical theory. Does anyone actually govern their actions in this way without experiencing negative consequences? On the contrary, we not only debate about ethics, but there are actions about which there is a great deal of agreement, murder in particular. This leads to the other observation that subjectivists fail to acknowledge, namely, people don't disagree about everything, and they give reasons to account for their common moral standards. Given these considerations, moral subjectivism is not a persuasive theory.

Unlike the subjectivist, the conventionalist argues that rather than moral judgments being mere expressions of individuals, they are expressions of approval and disapproval of social groups. For an action to be right it must be considered right by a particular social group, or culture. At first glance this seems to be a more persuasive view than subjectivism. However, this form of moral relativism confuses things in a similar way. Now moral judgments are simply relative to different groups instead of single individuals. To provide an example of this view let us say that your group believes that all members of humanity ought to be respected equally. However, a group of Neo-Nazis claim that Jews and people of color are inferior and should be killed. Who is right, your group or the Neo-Nazis? If there is no standard over and above both groups, then the judgments of each group are equally valid, since the rightness of the matter is merely a function of being based on beliefs held in common with a group—*any group and any action*. But is this reasonable? Like the subjectivist, the conventionalist argues that simply because there are sometimes different moral opinions from culture to culture, and group to group, no overarching standard exists. This does not necessarily follow. It *may be* that one explanation for these differences in opinion is that such a standard doesn't exist. However, it does not follow from any mere difference of opinion that there is no right or wrong to the matter, since it may be that one or more of the groups, even all of the groups, are wrong.

A more accurate view of the matter is that while there are cultural and group differences regarding moral matters, there is also a great deal of agreement. It may be that human understanding regarding morality may progress or even digress from culture to culture and historical period to period. In this text, we generally proceed with the assumption that there are impartial moral truths, and there seems to be very good reasons for thinking this way. Subjectivism and conventionalism may in part, be persuasive to some people because of some very real difficulties, both theoretical and practical when we engage in moral reasoning. Yet these difficulties do not justify the skepticism of the subjectivist position. In the next section we will address some of these difficulties.

1.5 Applying moral theories: Complex cases & Problems with Conflicting Principles

We often hear the view expressed that moral issues are not black and white, but involve shades of gray. There is some truth to this view. While there are some straightforward moral cases, moral issues are often complicated, and they often involve matters about which no general public consensus has been reached. Good examples of complex issues of this type are the controversies over abortion and stem-cell research. While one of the primary reasons that there is no current consensus about these issues is that people's perspectives are informed by different moral traditions, there are other reasons as well. At the heart of the abortion issue, there are questions regarding the moral status of a fetus. The problem is that there is no agreement over the moral status of a fetus, and this disagreement, in turn, perpetuates the question of whether or not a fetus has rights. Part of the problem is that defining what a person is involves more than a biological answer. This kind of issue is sometimes referred to as involving the **problem of ambiguity**. In ambiguous cases, it is sometimes possible to clarify what will be allowed under the law, but not to reach a general public consensus about the action in question.

Some cases also involve another complication, namely that of **opacity**.[5] Something opaque cannot be clearly seen through. Moral issues are opaque when there are unknowns. The current debate over stem-cell research presents a good example of opacity. Due to the fact that stem-cell technology has only recently developed, questions remain about how it can be applied, and what the long term impact of such applications could be. This makes it more difficult to decide whether or not the various applications of stem-cell research would be ethical. We shall see that some moral issues that confront businesses also involve ambiguities or opacity.

Another type of problem that sometimes occurs when dealing with difficult cases in ethics arises when we are confronted with **conflicting principles**. This occurs when we have two or more moral principles pulling us in different directions. In other words, cases where we feel like no matter which rule we follow, we end up doing the wrong thing because upholding one rule seems to lead us to violate the other equally binding rule.   The moral theories we examine in this book address this problem in various ways.

Finally, we need to take care that we do not assume that every moral issue is a difficult case. Moral controversies sometimes are caused not because the issue is ambiguous or opaque, nor because conflicting principles are involved, but by differences of opinion about **matters of fact** that apply to the situation under debate. Even people who share the same moral values sometimes disagree and it is commonly because they do not see the facts the same way. Debates like these can often be resolved with the introduction of new information. Often, one side or the other does not have a clear understanding of what occurred, or perhaps they don't have enough information to make the best decision. This leads to an important distinction regarding moral debates that is commonly overlooked. Some disagreements are matters of conflicting principle, while others are differences over matters of fact. Differences regarding matters of fact are more easily addressed since consensus can often be reached by simply coming to agreement over the facts. Matters of disagreement about principles are a much more difficult matter.   In these latter debates, opposing sides can come to agreement only if one side or the other gives up or revises its basic principles.

One of the great values of the study of business ethics is that we not only clarify our own moral perspectives, but we also learn more about the nature of moral conflicts, and how to correctly classify moral problems. This helps us become better moral decision makers, better managers and, as a result, more responsible citizens.

1.6 Ethics and Law

What is the relationship between **ethics** and the **law**? It has sometimes been claimed the two things have nothing to do with each other. Paradoxically, it has been argued by others that there is no difference and that being ethical is simply following the law. Upon reflection, however, it becomes clear that neither of these views is correct.

First, let us assume that ethics and law are entirely different. What does this claim mean? Does it mean that if someone breaks the law that she has not acted immorally? While this may sometimes be the case, it is not the case in respect to every action, or even most of the illegal actions committed. For example it is against the law to murder and to steal. We also generally believe that it is unethical to take the life of the innocent or take another person's property without reasonable cause. Surely then, there must be some relationship between law and ethics; the two things cannot be entirely unrelated since many of the acts that are illegal are also unethical. Second, let's assume instead that ethics and law are the same. While this would explain why many of the same actions are both illegal and considered unethical, it does not account for cases in which it may be ethical to actually break the law, nor does it account for the fact that some laws may not be ethical. For example, it is against the law in the United States to drive on left side of the road on two-way streets. However, surely it would be morally justified to do so if that were the only way to avoid a fatal collision. Likewise, before the enacting of civil rights laws, many women, African Americans, and other minorities suffered a much greater degree of institutional discrimination than they do today. This included state laws that were themselves unfairly discriminatory. How would we explain why we were justified in overturning such laws if the law and what is ethical is simply the same thing? On the contrary, laws themselves have to fair and ethical if they are to be good laws. By following this chain of reasoning, we can better understand the relationship between ethics and law and put into words why they can neither be completely different, nor entirely the same. The two areas of concern overlap. In fact, the laws in any given society seem to be a subset of the common moral customs of the society. We regulate those activities and practices that most affect our common rights, and that impact on public interests, including safety and property. Even in pluralistic societies, like that of the United States, there are great numbers of common moral customs. In most cases, actions that are legally permitted are permitted *because* it is believed that the actions are morally acceptable, or because it is believed that they are ambiguous matters of personal moral conscience that cannot be fairly legislated. Likewise, acts that are defined as illegal, such as murder and stealing, are typically defined as such and prohibited, *because* they are considered morally wrong and of such grave public consequence that they cannot be left to individual conscience. This approach also explains why laws change. Laws themselves are the products of human moral decisions. There can be ethical laws and unethical laws. Therefore, when discriminatory laws are repealed, it is *because* they are considered to be unfairly discriminatory and hence morally wrong.

Finally, there is one additional consideration that follows from our reflection on the nature of the relation between law and ethics. The two things overlap but are not identical.

Thus, as we consider what is moral and what is immoral, we will never assume that just because something is illegal, it is thereby unethical, nor can we assume that because something is legal that it is necessarily ethical. This consideration is very important to keep in mind because it is often thought that to be ethical in business, it is only necessary to operate in accordance to the law. However, this assumption merely amounts to the claim that the law and ethics are the same, an assumption we have shown to be implausible. Managers must consider what is legal, but they must also consider what is ethical. Thus, as we consider and attempt to solve moral problems in business, we must always consider both what is legal and what is moral as two separate but related concerns.

In the next chapter we will begin with a brief case study that will be used to illustrate the application of different moral theories. We will use the same case study in each of the remaining chapters to demonstrate how various moral theories tackle the same case differently. Each of the remaining chapters will focus on a particular moral theory. We will begin with the virtue theoretic approach, which is the oldest approach, and then turn our attention to more recent theories.

---

[1] Plato, *Apology*, G.M.A. Grube translation, reprinted in *The Trial and Death of Socrates*, 3rd ed., Hackett press, 2000, p. 39 (38b).

[2] The Exxon Valdez was a huge oil tanker which wrecked on a reef in 1989, spilling 10.8 million gallons of oil. It was the largest oil spill in U.S. history. The spill caused billions of dollars in damages and wreaked havoc on the environment. It was discovered that negligence was involved in the events leading up to the wreck.

[3] This definition is modeled after a similar approach offered by Leslie Stevenson in *Ten Theories of Human Nature,* 5th ed., Oxford University Press, 2008, pp. 3-5.

[4] Rachels, James, Stuart Rachels, *The Elements of Moral Philosophy*, 5th ed., McGraw Hill, New York, 2007, p. 13.

[5] Garrett, Thomas, Baillie, Harold, and Garrett, Rosellen, *Health Care Ethics*, 4th ed., Prentice Hall, 2001, pp. 10-12.

CHAPTER 2: THE VIRTUE THEORETIC APPROACH

2.1 The Concept of Virtue

We have all heard the expression "patience is a virtue." But what is a virtue? Clearly, the expression means that patience is a good thing, but why is it good? To answer this question, we would probably think about the sorts of problems that result from being impatient. For, example, if someone is striving to obtain a promotion, but lacks the required number of years of service, this person may give up too soon, if he or she is not patient. If someone is teaching a small child to walk, it would be unrealistic to help the child to its feet once and then expect the child to be walking with perfect balance on the following day. Certainly, if the person began shouting at the child for not walking perfectly, it could have a damaging effect on the child. From these examples, it seems that patience is some sort of quality that we can possess, or fail to adequately possess. We can also see from these two simple instances that whether someone possesses such a quality can influence how they actually behave. In the first example, the person gives up too soon and perhaps decides to leave his/her present employer. In the second case the person inappropriately shouts at a child thereby risking the child's psychological health. These actions are taken to express the opposite of the quality of patience, thus we view these people as impatient. The following is a common scenario in business that may open up further questions about other virtues:

Edna and Jackie "Other duties as Assigned":

Edna Forthright recently started working as an administrative assistant in Cleveland Packing Inc. Her supervisor, Jackie Ripper, has been training her on the company data-base and taking calls and orders, which are the bulk of her contracted responsibilities. Lately, however, Jackie has been asking Edna to do other kinds of tasks, some of which are beyond her experience and qualifications. Edna is growing increasingly concerned about making costly mistakes. Moreover, she has been having trouble getting her data entry done and returning calls because of the increased load exacted by her supervisor. Last Friday, Jackie called her into her office and seemed upset about Edna's performance. Edna finally confronted Jackie with her concerns about the new work she had been asked to do. Jackie replied by pulling out her contract, and pointed to the section of her job details, indicating that "5% may include other duties as assigned."

Does Edna have cause for concern? She is after all, a new employee. Is Jackie proceeding as a good manager? What virtues are at stake here? Most of us would suspect that Jackie is abusing the customary "other duties as assigned" clause in Edna's contract. And of course, Edna has cause for concern. Could it be that Jackie is giving Edna a portion of her own work? If both things are true, we would think that Edna was being treated unfairly (fairness) and the terms of her contract were being abused, which is a lack of due respect (respect). Moreover, if the other work Jackie is assigning her is her own, this would raise questions about Jackie's honesty, both in respect to Edna and to the company.

This manner of thinking about human qualities i.e. **virtues** and linking them to our actual actions is one of the most common and entrenched manners of thinking that westerners can readily grasp, whether or not they have taken an ethics course. Why? This is the **virtue-theoretic** approach. It is one of the oldest ways of thinking about ethics and is deeply entrenched in our language and moral concepts. Thus, virtue is as important today, as it was in 335 BCE, when the Greek Philosopher Aristotle, opened his school, the Lyceum.

Aristotle was not the only philosopher to study the nature of **arête**, meaning human excellence, or virtue. His teacher, the Greek philosopher Plato, had been working on this for some time. However, Aristotle was the first philosopher to attempt to give a systematic account of virtue, and he was one of the earliest moral philosophers with his own unique theory. Due to the enormous influence of Aristotle on western thought, we will begin our study of the virtue-theoretic approach to ethics by studying his view. We will then look at the way that virtue-theory developed and changed in the centuries that followed, especially under the influence of early Christian philosophers like St. Augustine of Hippo, and St. Thomas Aquinas, who will also be discussed in this chapter.

2.2 The Search for Happiness

Aristotle believed that every kind of thing in the universe, both living and non-living, had a specific nature, and purpose (**telos**), including human beings. This purpose determines the way each thing develops. Living things develop based on a form of pattern that seems determined in part by the kind of thing that it is. For example, consider the growth of an oak tree. The acorn falls to the ground. If the environment is right, it germinates, and grows. Again, if the environment is sufficiently nurturing, the tree grows into what it always potentially was as a seed, an oak tree. Aristotle thought of the fully developed oak as the realized purpose or goal of the life of the oak. Based on this background assumption, Aristotle began his treatise on morals, the *Nicomachean Ethics*, with an investigation into what kind of creature human beings are, and what their ultimate purpose might be. For Aristotle, humans are first and foremost, creatures of nature among other things in nature. We are rational and social animals. We are creatures that reason, and we seem to depend on one another to survive and to meet other wants and needs. Because we are rational, and have choices: we are to some extent free to determine for ourselves what our goals will be and how best to meet them. However, Aristotle asks, is there any *single* thing that *all* human beings seek? This thing, he hypothesized, would be our supreme good. Aristotle argues that our highest good was something that we all by nature seek, namely **happiness**, (eudemonia). First, he argues that because we notice all of our actions are aimed at some good, we are creatures that always pursue certain goals or ends. Next he argues that some activities seem more important to us than others because it is usually for the sake of these activities that we tend to obtain other goods and fulfill lesser needs. This positions him to ask the question, is there any one end towards which all of our other actions and choices are aimed? The following passages from *Nicomachean Ethics*, presents his argument.[1]

Every art and every investigation, and similarly every action and pursuit, is considered to aim at some good. Hence the good has been rightly defined as 'that which all things aim.' Clearly, however, there is some difference between the ends at which they aim: some are activities and others results distinct from the activities. Where there are ends distinct from actions, the results are by nature superior to the activities. Since there are many actions, arts and sciences, it follows that their ends are many too – the end of medical science is health; of military science, victory; of economic science, wealth. In the case of all skills of this kind that come under a single faculty – as a skill in making bridles or any other part of a horse's trappings comes under horsemanship, while this and every kind of military action comes under military science, so in the same way other skills are subordinate to yet others – in all these the ends of the directive arts are to be preferred in every case to those of the subordinate ones, because it is for the sake of the former that the latter are pursued also. It makes no difference whether the ends of the actions are the activities themselves or something apart from them, as in case of the sciences we have mentioned.

If then, our activities have some end which we want for its own sake, and for the sake of which we want all other ends—if we do not choose everything for the sake of something else (for this involves an infinite progression, so that our aim will be pointless and ineffectual)--it is clear that this must be the good, that is the supreme good. Does it not follow, then, that knowledge of the good is of great importance to us for the conduct of our lives? Are we not more likely to achieve our aim if we have a target? If this is so, we must try to describe at least in outline what the good really is, and by which of the sciences or faculties it is studied.

Aristotle is saying that if we examine our activities, forms of production, and the goals we try to achieve with them, there seems to be a hierarchy involved—we engage in some activities only to produce goods that support yet other activities. Some activities and goods seem to be only **extrinsically valuable**, that is, valuable as means to other things or activities, for example a horse's bridle used to ride horses. However, there must be some end to this, something that is both **intrinsically valuable**, valuable for its own sake, and for which everything else we do provides the means to this end, the supreme good. In his final remarks in the second passage he refers to there being a science that studies this good. Today we would call this ethics. In Aristotle's theory, he categorizes ethics as part of the larger study of politics, what we now call political science. In fact, in one of Aristotle's other works, *Politics*, he refers to humans as "***politikon zoon***," or political animals. Aristotle identifies this supreme good as happiness or "human well-being" as it is sometimes translated:

To resume. Since all knowledge and every pursuit aim at some good, what do we take to be the end of political science – what is the highest of all practical goods? Well, so far as the name goes there is pretty much general agreement. 'It is happiness,' say both ordinary and cultured people; and they identify happiness with living well and doing well or doing well. But when it comes to saying in what happiness consists, opinions differ…The former take it to be something obvious and familiar, like pleasure or money or eminence, and there are various other views; and often the same person often changes his opinion: when he falls ill he says that it is health, and when he is hard up that it is money. Conscious of their ignorance, most people are impressed by anyone who pontificates and says something that is over their heads.

Aristotle defines happiness in a two-fold fashion. First, it is an **activity of the soul**, and likewise a **sense of well-being** produced by this activity. This supreme happiness is the objective of a lifetime, and it is debatable whether we ever complete our pursuit. Nonetheless, according to Aristotle, it is our ideal. Aristotle warns about two pitfalls regarding the pursuit of happiness. First, it is common to pursue lesser goods, such as money, fame, power, or pleasure as if these were supreme ends. However, these are only ingredients in a larger activity of the soul that is greater in sum than all of these things. Second, this sense of well-being cannot be produced by actions that ignore the kind of being that we are, namely, political and social beings with complicated psychological needs in addition to biological ones. For humans to choose wisely, they must possess the character traits that enable them to perceive things correctly and do the right things in order to be fulfilled.

In these passages, not only has Aristotle argued that happiness is the goal that we all seek in life, but he has hinted at what he believes to be the best means to achieve our goal. Since we are rational creatures and exercise reason when we make our choices, seeking happiness successfully would depend on making good practical choices. He then considers what kind of human qualities seem to make us better decision makers, not only about our personal interests, but about the interests of our community as a whole. Aristotle saw ethics as a subject of the field of politics.   However, we must keep in mind that the term "politics" comes from the ancient Greek work **polis**, which is the word for city. Literally, it meant "the place of the people." So, for Aristotle, politics involves studying the principles that are the foundation of a good human society, a society in which we together pursue happiness, and fully develop as human beings.   In a harmonious society, the citizens must exercise reason well in order to make the right choices and enact the best laws. However, they will not do so unless they possess moral virtues, forms of excellence that will predispose them to act in the right way. If we, as citizens do not possess these, we tend to develop **vices** instead. A "vice" is the opposing extreme character trait which is recognized and defined in contrast to a virtue. For example, the opposite of the virtue of patience is impatience, of courage, cowardice.

Since virtues are human character traits, they cannot be acquired merely by study; rather it takes practical experience and practice to develop them.   According to Aristotle, possessing these virtues depends on developing the right **habits**. For example, someone who habitually lies is typically not trusted, because he/she is not truthful. In other words, this person lacks the virtue of truthfulness. One becomes truthful only by having been trained to tell the truth, learning also the consequences of failing to do so, and making a habit of telling the truth whenever it is appropriate to do so.

Aristotle explored a number of different virtues, including courage, temperance, moderation, generosity, magnificence, pride, the right degree of ambition, friendliness, truthfulness, the right sense of shame, and justice. It is readily apparent that we still value several of these character traits today; however, some of them don't seem to make sense outside of ancient Greek society.   For example, many would no longer think of pride as a virtue. In addition, in order to exercise the virtue of magnificence, one would have to be very wealthy, given that this virtue pertains to giving large gifts, perhaps what we would call today philanthropy, the act of extreme material generosity.   Contemporary supporters of the virtue theory approach have thus argued that some features of the morally good life may vary from culture to culture while some are common to all.   Philosophers have pointed out additional shortfalls in Aristotle's view of virtue as follows.

A common complaint raised against Aristotle's moral theory is the charge that his theory lacks the fundamental principle of impartiality due to the fact that Aristotle did not demand that his ethics and politics be egalitarian.   Aristotle was a man of his time, and ancient Greece was extremely class divided and patriarchal.   In many cities women had no independent rights, slavery was customary throughout the ancient world, and Greek cities tended to be xenophobic and had little concern for people who lived outside their own borders.   In contrast, the ideals of equality and a modicum of individual rights for *all human beings* are features demanded by most contemporary moral theories.   While this criticism is most likely true of Aristotle and ancient Greek culture, it is not clear to the author how this indicts Aristotle's moral theory. There is nothing in the structure of his theory that necessitates class division and inequality, or dictates that when social attitudes change, the conception of what is virtuous may evolve for the better.   Thus, the above criticism seems to be more of a criticism of Aristotle's historical era than anything that substantially challenges his theory.

Another criticism of Aristotle's theory pertains to his idea of the **golden mean**. Aristotle believed that virtues were associated with feelings and conduct which are the middle road between two extremes. The extremes themselves he associated with vices. Take for example, the virtue of moderation. Let's suppose that someone is on a diet. The person is a buffet dinner and must choose to take a healthy portion. Clearly they could take too little, or too much. Either would be opposite extremes. But a healthy diet includes taking the right amount. So, one can be immoderate by either taking too much or too little. However, many virtues do not seem to be so easily described as means between two extremes. In other words not all vices seem to be matters of doing or feeling too much or too little. While virtues such as moderation or courage seem to be matters of reaching a mean, there seem to be some actions that are always wrong in themselves. Using murder as an example—can you kill an innocent person too much or too little? Isn't it always wrong to commit this action? Aristotle himself points out that such actions are intrinsically wrong in *Nicomachean Ethics*; however, in the end he fails to fully address what accounts for them.

2.3 Christian Developments in Virtue Theory—Augustine and Aquinas

As previously mentioned, most contemporary moral theories emphasize the ideals of equality of rights and fair distribution of goods based on rational and non-arbitrary grounds. Similarly, we often believe that people possess some rights simply by being human. However, the ideal that such rights belong to all human beings did not begin to emerge in the west until centuries after Aristotle's death near the end of the Roman civilization. It is largely the work of early Christian philosophers that planted the seeds of these ideals in the western intellectual tradition.   The new concept that they introduced was that all men are equal under God and that despite any natural differences between them, they have an intrinsic value merely by being human.   This notion fundamentally changed the way ethical concepts and political expectations would develop in the centuries to come.[2]

Augustine was born in Tagaste on the coast of modern northern Africa in 354 CE.   His father was a pagan and his mother, Monica (later St. Monica) a Christian.   Augustine's moral theory is one of the first to embody the egalitarian ideal.   As a youth, Augustine was a pagan, and in his own estimation, lived a profligate and irresponsible life.   He studied rhetoric and philosophy in Rome and became a rhetorician.   Augustine was particularly interested in Plato's thought, which at the time was largely filtered through a group of philosophers known as Neo-Platonist.   They argued that everything in reality was ultimately one, and this highest ground of all reality was the Good itself, the source of all being and kinds of perfection.   This view had a profound influence on Augustine's intellectual development. It caused him to question many of the ideas of the Manichean's, a mystery religion popular in his time of which he had become a member.   Later, while in Rome he met Ambrose, a Christian bishop, who invited Augustine to join his circle of friends.   Through his debates with others in this circle, and his search for spiritual truth, Augustine converted to the religion of his mother, and pursued the priesthood in the church. In 395 CE, he was made Bishop of Hippo, a city near his birthplace. He became a prolific philosopher and theologian and his works comprise some of the most fundamental documents of Christianity.   He remained at Hippo until he was martyred in 430 CE when invading tribes burned his church.   He was later canonized a saint.

Much of Augustine's philosophy can be described as an attempt to combine what he believed to be true in Greek philosophy with Christian Scripture. Plato had postulated the ideal of the Good itself as the source of all being. For Augustine, the God of Abraham played this same role. He believed that God was the source of all being, truth, and perfection, including all moral perfection. However, Augustine's conception of God was the personal God of Christianity, not an abstract principle such as Plato's notion of the Good itself. While Augustine agreed with Plato that there must be a single purpose and form of perfection behind everything in the universe, and he argued like Aristotle, that in order for human beings to be happy they must seek the supreme good. He believed it was God, rather than nature, that constituted this highest good.

The purpose of our lives from Augustine's viewpoint is to repent our sins, seek reconciliation with God, and live a righteous life. He redefined virtue as living in accordance with the teachings of Jesus. Thus, for Augustine, virtues abstractly considered, are **forms of spiritual love**. Moreover, unlike Aristotle, he defined happiness as the activity of the soul in the life of faith, not simply an activity of rational excellence. In this way, reason is important to Augustine, but it is subordinate to the ends that are dictated by the object of Christian faith. Rebirth and reunion with God are the principle ends of the blessed life. "To reach God is Happiness itself." Augustine's argument for this view is presented in the following excerpt from his work entitled *Moral Behavior of the Catholic Church.*[3]

No one will question that virtue gives perfection to the soul. But it is the very proper subject of inquiry whether this virtue can exist by itself or only in the soul. Here again arises profound discussion, needing lengthy treatment; but perhaps my summary will serve the purpose. God will, I trust assist me, so that notwithstanding our feebleness, we may give instruction on these great matters briefly as well as intelligibly. In either case, whether virtue can exist by itself without the soul, or can exist only in the soul, undoubtedly in the pursuit of virtue the soul follows after something and this must be either the soul itself, or virtue, or something else. But if the soul follows after itself, it follows after a foolish thing; for before obtaining virtue it is foolish. Now the height of a follower's desire is to reach what it follows after. So the soul must either not wish to reach what it follows after, which is utterly absurd and unreasonable, or, in following after itself while foolish, it reaches the folly which it flees from. But if it follows after virtue in the desire to reach it, how can it follow what does not exist? Or how can it desire to reach what it already possesses? Either therefore, virtue exists beyond the soul, or if we are not allowed to give the name of virtue except to the habit and disposition of the wise soul, which can exist only in the soul, we must allow that the soul follows after something else in order that virtue be produced in itself; for neither by following after nothing, nor by following after folly, can the soul, according to my reasoning, attain to wisdom.

This something else then, by following after which the soul becomes possessed of virtue and wisdom, is either a wise man, or God. But we have already said it (the supreme good) must be something that we cannot lose against our will. No one can think it necessary to ask whether a wise man, supposing we are content to follow after him, can be taken away from us… God then remains, in following after whom we live well, and reaching whom we live both well and happily. (Parenthesis mine)

In addition to Augustine's arguing that God alone provides an adequate and worthy end for human pursuit, he focused on four cardinal virtues that he believed were fundamental for pursuing a good life: temperance, fortitude, justice, and prudence. However, these virtues are not, as Aristotle defined them, simply the means to attaining personal, material, or mental wellbeing. Instead, they define a religious way of life, ultimately aimed at life in the next world, not this world.

2.4 Aquinas and Further Developments

The next major stage of development in Christian virtue theory was developed by another churchman and scholar eight hundred years after the death of Augustine, during the late middle ages. Thomas Aquinas, born in Italy in 1225 CE, became the most prominent philosopher and theologian of the middle ages. Aquinas, following Augustine, argued that God was the ultimate source of all virtues and the basis of a moral life. However, Aquinas emphasized two other points as well. The Bible teaches that all men are equal under God. Therefore, Aquinas argued that the virtues are to be exercised in such a way that all enjoy the fruits of the righteous life. This is not to say that in actual practice, slavery and serfdom disappeared overnight in Europe, which we know was not the case. However, the seeds of a more egalitarian change in ethics were now taking root.

The second idea that Aquinas developed was borrowed explicitly from Aristotle, but Aquinas gave the idea a uniquely Christian twist. He argued that morals are based on reason and our rational insights into nature (just as Aristotle had argued); however, he argued that God is behind the ultimate design of both man and nature. Reason allows us to understand how things are supposed to be, and we are endowed with reason by God for this purpose. Thus, he concludes, morals are matters of **natural law**, discovered by reason, and are analogous to the natural laws of physics or chemistry. Unlike physical laws which govern matter, however, the moral law applied to agents with free will. Thus, humans have the power to either obey or to violate the moral law. Where do the natural laws come from? Aquinas reasoned that natural laws were in turn based on **divine law**, God's eternal plan for creation. To violate reason is therefore a misuse of God's gift. When one acts out of vice, one violates reason and

God's intended order in nature.   This philosophy remained dominant in the west until the late Renaissance. Even today, Thomism, as Aquinas's philosophy came to be called, remains at the heart of the moral perspectives of many Christians, especially in the Roman Catholic Church.

One of the difficulties that some philosophers find with the natural law approach is that it can be controversial defining what exactly God does or does not intend, and correlatively what is "natural" and "unnatural." This is reflected in public moral debates today over issues such as homosexuality and the permissibility of euthanasia. Natural law arguments are invoked by some to denounce homosexuality, yet by others, to defend the homosexual lifestyle. Similarly, natural law arguments have been used against suicide and active euthanasia. Nonetheless, many have argued that they have a natural right to die as they wish, especially if they are fatally ill and in great pain and distress.

By the beginning of the European Enlightenment (circa 1700's CE), philosophers began to seriously call into question the natural law approach, along with other aspects of Thomism. This was partly due to the concerns previously mentioned, but also because the classical and medieval view of nature was likewise coming into question.   After the discoveries of scientists such as Galileo, Kepler, and Isaac Newton, the classical conception of nature, going back to Aristotle, was largely overturned.   As a result, new moral theories, including secular moral theories, began to emerge.   It is important to note, however, that although the theorists we will explore in the remaining chapters develop views that differ from early virtue theorists, they do not altogether reject the importance of virtue.   They argue, instead, that the ancient and medieval accounts were incomplete. Many philosophers today still believe that the development of virtuous traits of character is vital to living a moral life.   Thus, in the context of

business ethics it is relevant to ask ourselves the question: What are the best character traits

for a manager?   We can easily see from the case study of Edna Forthright and Jackie Ripper

that people who lack certain virtues do not, in fact make good managers.

---

[1] Aristotle, *Nicomachean Ethics*, Penguine Books, New York.

[2] Navia, Lewis E, Ethics and the Search for Value, Prometheus Books, Buffalo, New York, 1980, p. 153.

[3] Augustine, "The Moral Behavior of the Catholic Church," from *The Essential Augustine*, Hackett Press, Indianapolis, 1978, p. 156, Part 6.

CHAPTER 3: UTILITARIANISM

3.1 The British Enlightenment

The Scottish Philosopher, David Hume (1711-1776) proposed a radically new approach to defining what is valuable. In Hume's view all things are considered in terms of their *utility* or usefulness for fulfilling human desires. Hume, a skeptic and avid atheist, rejected all other approaches to value, classical and religious. Hume was one of the most prominent figures of the early European Enlightenment. In 18th Century England, the new rising stars in philosophy and science were bent on progress, which they believed required a complete break with Thomism. They championed a new conception of philosophy and the sciences, free of the influences of religious traditions. By the middle of the 19th Century, the modern nation state started to emerge following the French revolution and the Napoleonic wars. In the Americas, a new country was established based on a constitution that emphasized personal liberty, the division of church and state, equality, and the pursuit of happiness. The western countries entered the industrial revolution and the mercantile economy began to evolve into capitalism. U.S. Americans fought a bloody civil war, ending slavery in the western world.[1]

Amidst all of these changes, progressives like British philosopher Jeremy Bentham (1748-1832) and his pupil, John Stuart Mill, developed a new approach to ethics that would make a decisive break with past tradition. Building on Hume's idea of **utility**, they argued for a theory called **Utilitarianism**. Due to the fact that their ideas were highly influential in newly developing political and economic policies throughout Europe and in America, no other moral theory has perhaps had as much impact on the modern world. John Mill, a prominent historian and economist, was one of Bentham's followers. His son, John Stuart Mill, inherited their progressive social causes and continued to champion the theory. In his essay *Utilitarianism* (1861) Mill defends the theory from its critics. However, Mill's approach changed certain aspects of Bentham's original theory. For this reason, we will look at Bentham and Mill's approaches separately. Bentham's version of this theory is commonly referred to as classical or **act utilitarianism**, while Mill's version is now considered by many to have contained a new approach later referred to as **rule utilitarianism.**

3.2 Bentham's Approach

The foundational claim of Bentham's theory is that human happiness is of supreme value. At first glance this seems a restatement of Aristotle's position. However, Bentham did not define happiness in the same way. Recall from the last chapter that Aristotle argued that happiness could not be reduced to any one kind of human good. Bentham argued instead that all happiness was reducible to one type of good, namely "pleasure." Hence, he argued that there was only one good, pleasure, and only one evil, pain. This view is called **hedonism**, an approach that goes back to the ancient Greek philosopher Epicurus and his followers. Subsequent philosophers who held this view were commonly referred to as **Epicureans**. While contemporary philosophers have developed non-hedonistic versions of utilitarianism, it is the early hedonistic versions that have had the most influence in contemporary economic and political thought. Bentham proposed one ultimate principle for achieving the good; the **Principle of Utility**. This principle requires that we always choose the actions or policies that have the best consequences for the greatest number of stakeholders concerned. By "best consequences," however, Bentham meant the course of action which produces the most pleasure, and the least amount of pain, for the greatest number of persons. On the whole, he argued that actions and social policies should benefit the greatest number possible. While this might not seem to be a very radical idea, it is important to remember that Bentham was writing in the 18th century, and as many philosophers and historians have pointed out, it is what this view omits that is most revolutionary.[2] Ethics are not based on Christian scripture, and all references to God and divine law are absent.

Bentham believed that his hedonistic theory of value was superior to other views because he argued that it had a scientific basis. However, most philosophers and psychologists now find some of his assumptions somewhat naïve. For example, Bentham believed that we could quantify units of pleasure and pain. Thus, in theory one could calculate and measure how pleasurable or painful a given course of action would be, and be able to make policy based on experience with such results. A little reflection shows the main problem with this view. There is a large subjective element in our experiences of pleasure and pain. Thus, how could such experiences ever be quantified as if they were similar to quantities of liquids or solids? In John Stuart Mill's approach, this aspect of the theory is conspicuously missing. Apparently, the young Mill saw the same problem and did not think it was a necessary element in the theory. Most contemporary utilitarians agree that Bentham's **hedonic calculus**, is unfounded, and can be rejected, without undermining the rest of his moral theory.

3.3 John Stuart Mill and the Greatest Happiness Principle

When John Stuart Mill published *Utilitarianism* in 1861 he refocused and clarified the theory in several ways.   In this section we will explore these changes in regard to the foundation of the theory, its single principle, and in respect to how Mill thought the principle ought to be applied when we decide how to act and create policies.

First, Mill argued that while Bentham was right in thinking that pleasure was the sole good, and pain the sole evil, he was wrong in thinking that all pleasures are the same.   Mill, argued that there are *higher* and *lower* pleasures; not necessarily in respect to their intensity, but in regard to their quality.   Mill explains this when he attempts to defend hedonism in the following passage.[3]

> Now such a theory excites in many minds and among them in some of the most estimable in feeling and purpose, inveterate dislike.   To suppose that life has (as they express it) no higher end than pleasure—no better and nobler object of desire and pursuit—they designate as utterly mean and groveling, as a doctrine worthy only of swine, to whom the followers of Epicurus were, at a very early period, contemptuously likened; and modern holders of the doctrine are occasionally made the subject of equally polite comparisons by its German, French, and English assailants.
>
>   When thus attacked, the Epicureans have always answered that it is not they, but their accusers, who represent human nature in a degrading light, since the accusation supposes human nature to be capable of no pleasures except those of which swine are capable.

Mill defends the Epicureans by arguing that humans are capable of far more than swine, both in terms of the range of our experience as well as the qualities of our pleasures. He continues:

Human beings have faculties more elevated than the animal appetites and, when once made conscious of them, do not regard anything as happiness which does not include their gratification. I do not, indeed, consider the Epicureans to have been by any means faultless in drawing out their scheme of consequences from the utilitarian principle. To do this in any sufficient manner, many Stoic, as well as Christian, elements require to be included. But there is no known Epicurean theory of life which does not assign to the pleasures of the intellect, of the feelings and imagination, and of the moral sentiments a much higher value as pleasures than those of mere sensation. It must be admitted, however, that utilitarian writers in general have placed the superiority of mental over bodily pleasures chiefly in the greater permanency, safety, uncostliness etc., of the former—that is, in their circumstantial advantages, rather than in their intrinsic nature. And on all these points utilitarians have fully proved the case; but they might have taken the other and, as it may be called, higher ground with entire consistency. It is quite compatible with the principle of utility to recognize the fact that some kinds of pleasure are more desirable and more valuable than others. It would be absurd that, while in estimating all other things quality is considered as well as quantity, the estimation of pleasure should be supposed to depend on quantity alone.

We can see in this passage, the clear break with Bentham's focus on the *quantity* of pleasures. Mill is arguing instead that there are natural *qualitative* differences in regard to various pleasures, and that some are more valuable than others. However, we need to consider how pleasures, in this view could be distinguished from one another in respect to quality. If there is a difference, let us say, between the pleasure of watching an opera, and the pleasure of eating a Bologna sandwich, then how can we explain why the former pleasure is commonly taken to be more gratifying and "higher" than the latter. Apparently, it is not because of any *intrinsic* difference, because as Mill himself states, pleasures are no different from one another in this respect. So, how do we understand a difference in the quality of pleasures? Mill's answer to this question is interesting. He appeals to the general opinions of the majority. In this respect his argument is not conclusive. It is rather a purely popular appeal. He states:

> If I am asked what I mean by difference of quality in pleasures, or what makes one pleasure more valuable than another, merely as a pleasure, except its being greater in amount, there is but one answer. Of the two pleasures, if there be one to which all or almost all who have experience of both give a decided preference, irrespective of any feeling of moral obligation to prefer it, that is the more desirable pleasure.

While deferring to popular appeal seems to side-step the problem we have already mentioned, it really only makes the issue more complicated.   Does the fact that any group of people happen to prefer something necessarily mean that the thing they happen to prefer *is better* than another thing?   Take a logically analogous example. Does the fact that most, if not all, people in the ancient world believed that the world was like a flat disc, make it the case that the world really is flat?   Simply put, popular opinion can be wrong.   Mere popular agreement about a belief does not make that belief true. Most philosophers today agree that Mill failed to adequately defend his distinction between higher and lower pleasures.

In regard to the second level of the theory, Mill further clarified the principle of utility. Mill refers to it as the "**greatest happiness principle**" and gave it a more precise formulation. According to this principle, "actions are right in proportion as they tend to promote happiness; wrong as they tend to produce the reverse of happiness," for the greatest number of sentient beings.[4] Before exploring how Mill intended the principle to be applied, we need to clarify two points about this principle.   First of all, the principle does not require that everyone who is affected by an action or policy benefit equally, and second, it does not even require that everyone benefit at all—it only requires that *most* who are affected by an action or policy are benefited. Hence, the objective is to maximize as much happiness as possible numerically, for the greatest number of beings.

Finally, in regard to the application of the theory, Mill makes some other very important provisions. Mill makes it clear that while the principle need not be exercised such that everyone is benefited, or equally benefited all of the time; in order for it to be a moral principle, it must be applied *impartially* all of the time. This means that in the consideration of people's interests, every individual counts as one. Moreover, every **sentient being**, which is every being that is capable of feeling pleasure and feeling pain, counts in the moral equation and must be considered, including non-human animals, albeit they need not be considered equally. As an aside, Bentham was one of the most prominent philosophers to use this point to argue against cruelty to animals. A second clarification regarding how to apply the principle concerns what Mill believed to be the important part of any course of action we choose. He argued that the only morally relevant aspects of an action are the consequences of the action. This view is called **consequentialism.** This claim, as we will see in the next section, raises several concerns for non-utilitarians. Mill argues that our motives and our intentions have nothing to do with whether or not an action is moral or immoral. To many people this claim seems hard to accept. We will address further challenges to utilitarianism in the next section. We will end this section with an application of the theory.

In the case of Edna Forthright and Jackie Ripper discussed in chapter two, we noted that a virtue-theorist would begin by examining the various virtues or vices that the stakeholders in that situation displayed. Jackie appeared to be treating Edna unfairly, selfishly abusing Edna by increasing her work load for her own benefit, without due respect for Edna's feelings and interests. While it is likely that in this case, a utilitarian would agree with a virtue theorist's assessment, that Jackie had done some wrong, they would approach the case in an entirely different manner. The utilitarian would ask whether the greatest happiness for the greatest number of persons affected was being served by Jackie's actions. We would need to weigh all of the consequences, both the good and the bad against one another. Clearly, the actual and potential negative consequences of Jackie's action outweighs any benefits that Jackie alone is enjoying, because not only is Edna made unhappy by the additional work, but we must also recall that her actual job duties are suffering as a result. The company, Cleveland Packing Inc., depends on Edna's job functions, and the company constitutes a far greater number of stakeholders who are adversely affected by Jackie's managerial practices than the single individual, Jackie who alone appears to be benefited. Thus, an impartial application of the principle of utility determines that Jackie's practice of giving Edna increasingly more work that falls outside her contracted duties, and which exceeds the typical percentages that apply to other duties as assigned, is morally wrong. Jackie's action results in more pain than any happiness it is creating.

The reader should notice that in the utilitarian evaluation of this case there is no consideration of Jackie's motives or intentions. To Mill, and later utilitarians, such considerations are irrelevant to the issue of morality, which is determined by considering the consequences of actions on the greatest number of stakeholders and nothing else. In other words, the ends either justify the means or they do not. Why do utilitarians believe that consequences are the only thing that matter? One reason why Mill embraced this idea was that he was an *empiricist*. An empiricist is a person who believes that all knowledge comes from sense perception and inner perception, the latter being the operations of the mind itself. While Mill did not disbelieve that people had motives and intentions for their actions, he noted that these matters are not publically observable and thus, not verifiable. Only the material results of our actions (the consequences) are publicly observable. Thus, he reasoned only the consequences of our actions are the basis for making objective decisions about the morality of our actions. Like Bentham, Mill believed that this was a more scientific approach.

In the next section, we will address some of the more serious contemporary criticisms of utilitarianism as well as some of the responses that utilitarians use to defend their theory. Many of these debates are at the heart of several business ethics problems today, not only because of the prominence of utilitarian moral views in philosophy, but because of similar utilitarian approaches common in economics and legal philosophy.

3.4 Recent Debates and Rule Utilitarianism

Criticism 1: The Greatest Happiness Principle is incompatible with our expectations about individual rights and justice.

The first criticism focuses on the utilitarian assumption that the only thing that matters in determining whether an action is right or wrong is the outcome of the action.

Obviously, if it were the case that consequences were not the only factor we must consider, then the utilitarian position would be unsupportable. The following scenario is a noted example cited by many moral philosophers today to illustrate this criticism. It was written by H.J. McCloskey in 1965 during the burgeoning of the civil rights movement. In regard to the language that McCloskey uses in the example, it is important to consider the decade in which he was writing.

> Suppose a utilitarian were visiting an area in which there was racial strife, and that during this visit, a Negro rapes a white woman, and that race riots occur as a result of the crime, white mobs, with the connivance of the police, bashing and killing Negroes, etc. Suppose too that our utilitarian is in the area of the crime when it is committed such that his testimony would bring about the conviction of a particular Negro (But not necessarily the actual perpetrator). If he knows that a quick arrest will stop the riots and lynchings, surely as a Utilitarian, he must conclude that he has a duty to bear false witness in order to bring about the punishment of an innocent person.[5] *Material in parenthesis mine.*

The practice that McClosky is highlighting is called "scapegoating," and his point is that utilitarianism appears to condone bearing false witness and the imprisonment or even execution of an innocent person if the expected consequences seem to merit this. Most people would recognize that this violates our concept of justice as well as the civil rights of the individual "sacrificed" for the good of the majority. Why should an innocent man be punished for a crime he did not commit? McClosky then suggested the obvious implication of his example. Utilitarianism is at odds with our belief that individual rights must be protected. In Mill's conception of the theory, the *ends justify the means in all cases*. The theory ignores the *nature of the means* (the actions) committed to achieve

44

the greatest good for the greatest number.   Do the ends always justify the means? Any

means?

Reply to Criticism 1:   Our traditional concept of rights is in error

J.J.C. Smart, a prominent contemporary utilitarian, argued that examples like the

McClosky scenario overemphasize the importance of our common sense notions about

individual rights.   In fact, Smart argues that in such cases common sense may be wrong.

While Smart does not deny that such rights are important, he argues that there may be

compelling enough reasons to override even the life and interests of innocent

individuals in some circumstances.[6]   In regard to the McClosky example, he might say

that we should focus on all of the consequences, including the innocent people whose

lives will be saved, or secured from injury, because of the sacrifice of the one innocent.

Readers will have to consider for themselves whether this is a convincing reply.

**Criticism 2: Utilitarianism is incompatible with our expectations regarding promises
and secrets.**

How important are promises?   How important are secrets?   A little reflection

reveals that both promises and secrets involve various kinds of agreements, sometimes

written and explicit, but at other times such agreements are natural, and thus unwritten

and simply understood.   We normally take our promises very seriously. And there are

secrets that not only protect individuals, but entire nations.   However, can utilitarianism

maintain the integrity of our promises and secrets?   Take the following example.   First,

let's assume, a person makes a promise to his spouse that they will have dinner

together on their anniversary.   On the evening of their anniversary, he is suddenly called by his father and told that his mother has been in a serious auto accident and that he must come to the hospital at once. Now in this case we might consider breaking a promise to be acceptable since the situation is extraordinary and the stakes are extremely high. However, now contrast this example with another one with different stakes. Let's assume that on the evening of the anniversary the fellow is called instead by a group of close buddies who have not seen him in years. Moreover, they will only be in town one more night and have tickets to the ball game. They really want him to come. He feels obligation to his spouse, but if he breaks his promise he may enjoy the company of his friends and the ball game, even if he does not get to enjoy the company of his spouse for dinner. If he breaks his promise, his spouse will likely be very unhappy. But the spouse *only counts as one*. There are six friends who would enjoy his presence, and even if he is unhappy with his decision to break his date with his spouse, the happiness of the greater number outweighs his unhappiness and that of his spouse. Therefore, it would seem that utilitarianism would *require him to break his promise*, even in cases where the stakes are very marginal. We can easily see that similar examples can be cited regarding secrets, in which secrets are revealed only for marginal gains. If promises can be broken, or secrets revealed for only slight gains in utility, then in principle, what promise or secret could ever be considered sacred or secure? We would probably say that the nature of the promise to the spouse is much more important than the opportunity of pleasing his friends, but to make this claim one has to appeal to factors other than a simple calculation of the amount of pleasure created by the action in contrast the pain for the greatest number. Thus, utilitarianism does not seem to be able to explain the sanctity of promises and secrets.

Reply to criticism 2: Act vs. Rule Utilitarianism

John Hospers was a contemporary philosopher who defended a version of utilitarianism referred to as **rule utilitarianism.** Hospers argued persuasively that Mill's essay is commonly misread, because critics oversimplified how the greatest happiness principle is to be applied. He then distinguished between two types of utilitarianism, **act utilitarianism,** which he attributed to Bentham, and rule utilitarianism, which he argued was implicit in Mill's version. Hospers claimed that the criticisms that the theory is inconsistent with our notions of promises and secrets, and that it is inconsistent with our notions of justice may be valid in respect to act utilitarianism, but not valid for rule utilitarianism, which he argued is truer to Mill's essay, in intent if not in word.[7]

Act utilitarians argue that we should apply the principle of utility to *every* action that we consider. Thus, each time we consider acting, we should consider all of the possible consequences in regard to how much pleasure and pain will be produced for the greatest number by our action. In addition to the fact that this demand seems incredibly impractical, Hosper's problem with this view is that it ignores the fact that what Mill had in mind was that the principle of utility be applied to practices and policies, in other words *rules*, with a view toward long-term gains in happiness, not short-term gains for the stakeholders immediately affected. In contrast, rule utilitarians, like Mill and Hospers, argue that we should apply the principle of utility to rules instead of actions. Once a type of practice or kind of action has been established to result in the most utility *as a rule*, then, as a matter of policy, such practices and actions should be performed. We can see the difference this provision makes by reconsidering the previous example of the promise of the man and his spouse to go out to dinner on their anniversary. In order to go out with his friends, he must break a promise to his spouse. The act utilitarian would do so, because more people would be pleased by this decision and only one person entirely disappointed, namely the man's spouse. However, this approach does not fully calculate the long-term consequences that would result if everyone acted in this way– the real question, according to Hospers, is not what the results of breaking this one promise at this time will be, *but whether the practice of breaking promises, as a rule*, will lead to the best results. Put this way, we can see that as a rule, making promises with no intention of keeping them, or breaking promises for marginal results, will not as a rule, promote the greatest good for the greatest number. Therefore, argues Hospers, such acts as a rule are unethical.

Criticism 3: The Hedonism Fallacy— Is pleasure the only good?

We should recall that Aristotle refused to reduce happiness to pleasure. For Aristotle there are actions and practices that we can perform that are good in themselves, irrespective of the goods they produce, and human happiness involves such activities, not merely taking pleasure in the goods they produce. This next criticism further illustrates why Aristotle argued this point.

Do we value things only insofar as we find them pleasurable, or do we also find things pleasurable *because* we believe they are valuable? Hedonism assumes that only the first proposition is true. It claims that we only value things because of pleasure. In other words, nothing other than pleasure has value, and everything else only has extrinsic value. There are two problems with this view: first, it implies that nothing other than pleasure has value in itself (intrinsic value), and second, it does not seem to be consistent with the way people actually experience the things that they value.

Consider a person's feelings for her spouse or child. Granted, she may take pleasure in their company. However, does that mean that the pleasure she takes is the only thing that she values about her spouse or child? Do her spouse and child have needs and value that are separate from her own and which are just as important as her own? We typically look at persons as having intrinsic value and dignity that is not dependent upon the pleasure that they afford others. In fact, we often say that we take pleasure in our spouse or child in great measure because we value them as they are, and not merely as a means to our own private ends. So, many philosophers have concluded that hedonism, upon which classical utilitarianism is based, gets things backwards. Pleasure, as Aristotle argued, cannot be the only good. To assume that it is mistakes the effect of enjoying what we value for the reasons that we value it in the first place.

Replies to Criticism 3

Some utilitarians, like J.J.C. Smart still adhere to the classical version with its hedonistic assumptions about value. However, they have no clear argument to defend the theory against the charge we just explored. At best they have argued that the question regarding whether there are other intrinsic goods other than pleasure has never been resolved. However, we should ask, if this is so, then why assume that pleasure is the only good, since it raises so many practical difficulties regarding our moral concepts?

Other utilitarians have abandoned hedonism, but retained the consequentialist position. They claim that instead of happiness, we should seek to maximize human welfare, more broadly defined. Still others argue that we should maximize human preferences. Nonetheless, all utilitarians argue that it is the consequences of actions alone that determine their moral value. This claim is a defining feature of the utilitarian position. In the next chapter we will examine the moral theory of Immanuel Kant, who argues that because of this, the utilitarian approach entirely misses the true basis of moral value.

---

[1] Rachels, James, Rachels, Stuart, *The Elements of Moral Philosophy*, 5th ed., McGraw Hill, 2007, p. 89.

[2] Ibid, p. 91.

[3] Mill, John Stuart, *Utilitarianism*, Macmillan Library of Liberal Arts, Prentice Hall, 1957.

[4] Ibid, p.10.

[5] Rachels, Ibid, p. 103. McCloskey's example first appeared in the journal Inquiry, 1965.

[6] Smart, J.J.C. and Williams, Bernard, Utilitarianism: For and Against, Cambridge, Cambridge University Press, 1973, p. 68.

[7] Hospers, John, See "Rule-Utilitarianism," in *Moral Philosophy: A Reader*, ed. Louis P. Pojman, 3rd ed. (Indianapolis: Hackett Publishing Company, Inc., 2003), 157-167. Hospers' article is reprinted from his book *Human Conduct: An Introduction to the Problem of Ethics*.

CHAPTER FOUR: Kant and the Deontological Approach

During the European Enlightenment the utilitarians, like Bentham and Mill were not the only philosophers who were rethinking traditional approaches to ethics. Long before J.S. Mill published his essay on "Utilitarianism," German philosopher Immanuel Kant (1724-1804) advanced his own theory which challenged both the Aristotelian and consequentialist approaches to ethics. Kant argued that the Aristotelian approach was flawed because it focused on happiness as the supreme end of human action. Kant argued that our concept of happiness was too open to subjective interpretation, to be considered a proper end for our moral conduct. The result, he argued made moral decisions too subjective and prone to selfish partiality. Similarly, Kant rejected the hedonistic view of happiness, as well as the view that the consequences of actions are the only thing that gives our actions moral value. Instead, Kant introduced a different approach, now called **deontological** theory, after the Greek term *deon* meaning duty. Kant's begins his theory with an analysis of the concept of moral duty which he believed contains the basic principles of morality. Kant's theory has been immensely influential, especially in respect to the contemporary discussion about rights in moral and legal philosophy. Kant is noted as both the inventor of the deontological approach and as a primary example of a **moral absolutist**, that is, someone who believes that there are moral absolutes that all human beings should observe. As in the previous chapter, we will discuss key elements of Kant's theory in the first sections of the chapter and then discuss criticisms and responses.

The final section will briefly look at the work of contemporary deontologist, W.D. Ross, who introduced several useful revisions of Kant's theory.

4.1 Goodwill and the Foundation of Moral Conduct

One of the primary differences between Kant's approach and that of the classical and consequentialist approaches to ethics is the manner in which Kant defined what is of greatest value. Kant argues that the ultimate goal of all of our actions, insofar as they are moral actions, is <u>not</u> some good that we are aiming at beyond those actions (e.g. happiness); rather the goal is to perform actions of a particular kind based on the right kind of intent. Kant introduces the foundation of his moral theory in the opening chapter of his work *Groundwork for the Metaphysics of Morals.* [1]

Nothing can possibly be conceived in the world, or even out of it, which can be called good, without qualification, except a good will. Intelligence, wit, judgement, and the other talents of the mind, however they may be named, or courage, resolution, perseverance, as qualities of temperament, are undoubtedly good and desirable in many respects; but these gifts of nature may also become extremely bad and mischievous if the will which is to make use of them, and which, therefore, constitutes what is called character, is not good. It is the same with the gifts of fortune. Power, riches, honour, even health, and the general well-being and contentment with one's condition which is called happiness, inspire pride, and often presumption, if there is not a good will to correct the influence of these on the mind, and with this also to rectify the whole principle of acting and adapt it to its end. The sight of a being who is not adorned with a single feature of a pure and good will, enjoying unbroken prosperity, can never give pleasure to an impartial rational spectator. Thus a good will appears to constitute the indispensable condition even of being worthy of happiness.

There are even some qualities which are of service to this good will itself and may facilitate its action, yet which have no intrinsic unconditional value, but always presuppose a good will, and this qualifies the esteem that we justly have for them and does not permit us to regard them as absolutely good. Moderation in the affections and passions, self-control, and calm deliberation are not only good in many respects, but even seem to constitute part of the intrinsic worth of the person; but they are far from deserving to be called good without qualification, although they have been so unconditionally praised by the ancients. For without the principles of a good will, they may become extremely bad, and the coolness of a villain not only makes him far more dangerous, but also directly makes him more abominable in our eyes than he would have been without it.

A good will is good not because of what it performs or effects, not by its aptness for the attainment of some proposed end, but simply by virtue of the volition; that is, it is good in itself, and considered by itself is to be esteemed much higher than all that can be brought about by it in favour of any inclination, nay even of the sum total of all inclinations. Even if it should happen that, owing to special disfavour of fortune, or the niggardly provision of a step-motherly nature, this will should wholly lack power to accomplish its purpose, if with its greatest efforts it should yet achieve nothing, and there should remain only the good will (not, to be sure, a mere wish, but the summoning of all means in our power), then, like a jewel, it would still shine by its own light, as a thing which has its whole value in itself. Its usefulness or fruitfulness can neither add nor take away anything from this value. It would be, as it were, only the setting to enable us to handle it the more conveniently in common commerce, or to attract to it the attention of those who are not yet connoisseurs, but not to recommend it to true connoisseurs, or to determine its value.

As noted in the previous passage, Kant believed that a quality of our will, namely **a will good in itself** is the only supreme good. All other goods, including happiness, cannot be said to be good without qualification. If a person possessed certain temperaments and virtues, for example courage and self-control, there is no guarantee that in her pursuit of happiness, that she will exercise these virtues for moral purposes. Thus, we can imagine a thief who is even more able because of her self-control and courage. A virtue-theorist might point out to Kant, that a virtuous person must also possess fairness and justice; therefore, they would not become a thief. Kant argues that it is not only necessary to possess wisdom to know when and how to act, but also to act for the right reasons; reasons that proceed from a benevolent disposition or good will. Another reason Kant approaches ethics in this fashion is that he recognizes a problem in human nature that had previously been addressed by Aristotle. We sometimes know what we should do, but fail to do it.   Why?   Aristotle referred to this as *akrasia*, or **weakness of the will**.   Kant therefore argues that in order to be moral, we must *make* our conduct comply with rules that we know are based on moral reasons.   However, what kinds of rules are best?

4.2 Moral Maxims and the Categorical Imperative

Kant believed that moral rules were absolute.   Thus, for example, he believed that it is never right to tell a lie, even for a good cause.   Kant believed that we must rationally concede that this is true after we examine the concept of **moral duty**.   When we think about doing something, out of a sense of duty, that is, obligation, do we think to ourselves, "I don't feel like doing this and I think I will blow it off?"   Clearly we sometimes do this, but if we had a genuine obligation, then we would normally think that we have done something wrong, in other words, we failed in our duty.   Kant argues that moral rules are based on obligations, not our feelings our mere whims and desires.   Kant makes a distinction between two types of rules, **hypothetical and categorical**. The former are rules that are dependent upon our private desires and interests.   These rules are reasonable for me to follow, but only if I want to do something that requires these rules in the first place.   For example, if a person wants to become a great painter, then she *ought* to practice techniques in painting.   Notice that the sense or force of the "ought" in this example is not absolute.   I would only be rationally compelled to practice my painting techniques, if I wanted to be a painter in the first place. However, Kant asks, are our moral rules the same as these?   For example, if we are obliged not to harass one another, does that sense of obligation depend on our whims or feelings? Hence, could a person morally say: "I will respect you and not harass you, but only if I desire not to do so in the first place?" Clearly, we do not think of moral rules in this way. Kant claims that moral rules carry an *imperative* force, like commands. As such, they are always to be followed. If it is wrong to harass others, then we should never do it. He addresses this distinction in the following passage.

Now all imperatives command either hypothetically or categorically. The former represent the practical necessity of a possible action as means to something else that is willed (or at least which one might possibly will). The categorical imperative would be that which represented an action as necessary of itself without reference to another end, i.e., as objectively necessary.

Since every practical law represents a possible action as good and, on this account, for a subject who is practically determinable by reason, necessary, all imperatives are formulae determining an action which is necessary according to the principle of a will good in some respects. If now the action is good only as a means to something else, then the imperative is hypothetical; if it is conceived as good in itself and consequently as being necessarily the principle of a will which of itself conforms to reason, then it is categorical.

Thus the imperative declares what action possible by me would be good and presents the practical rule in relation to a will which does not forthwith perform an action simply because it is good, whether because the subject does not always know that it is good, or because, even if it know this, yet its maxims might be opposed to the objective principles of practical reason.

Accordingly the hypothetical imperative only says that the action is good for some purpose, possible or actual. In the first case it is a problematical, in the second an assertorial practical principle. The categorical imperative which declares an action to be objectively necessary in itself without reference to any purpose, i.e., without any other end, is valid as an apodeictic (practical) principle.

By "apodictic," Kant means that moral rules are categorical imperatives. They oblige us categorically, so that obligations are strictly necessary; they are not dependent on any purpose or desire that we might or might not have. Moral rules are not hypothetical imperatives.

In addition to having absolute force, Kant believed that moral rules were based on reason alone. Unlike religious moral perspectives that might claim that there are moral absolutes based on scripture or the will of God, Kant believed that what was moral for one person was moral for all because all human beings have a common cognitive structure. We are all rational beings with a common human nature. Therefore, Kant argued that moral rules must also be **universal** in scope and apply to everyone equally. The absolute and universal qualities of moral rules are captured in Kant's idea of the supreme moral law, or the moral categorical imperative: **"Act only on that maxim whereby thou canst at the same time will that it should become a universal law."** [2] We can think of this as a master rule that sets forth conditions for any of our specific moral rules e.g., do not lie, cheat, steal, etc., as well as our **moral maxims**. Moral maxims are the reasons for a particular action under moral consideration. These reasons capture our specific intentions in a particular situation. Thus, for example, let us say that a person is considering calling into work and telling a lie, that he is ill, so that he can go fishing with his friend. The person's maxim would be, "any time I desire not to go to work in order to do a more enjoyable activity, I may lie to my employer." Can this maxim meet the conditions of the categorical imperative, that is, could we will such a maxim to be universal law, making it morally permissible for anyone to choose accordingly for this reason? Clearly we could not will that such a maxim be a universal law for it would undermine our work ethic and no one could be counted on to do their work responsibly. Thus, since such a maxim is logically inconsistent with the basic aims of our employment, an action based on it is morally wrong.

This example raises another issue for Kant. Kant is well known for his position regarding lying. Kant was an absolutist and believed that moral rules should be followed always and without exception, *regardless of the consequences.* Thus, he believed that it was never permissible to tell a lie. We will address this claim later in the chapter. At this point, it is important to note that Kant believed that the consequences of actions have nothing to do with their moral worth. Thus, Kant believes it is the reason behind our actions, alone, including the intent behind our actions, which determines whether our actions are moral or immoral. From Kant's perspective, the only way to consistently act out of good will is to act in accordance to the moral law, regardless of the consequences. This insures that we will not be led astray by our selfish inclinations. Going back to the example above, the fellow may not want to go to work, and want to go fishing. However, he knows that he has a duty to go to work. He is not really ill, and if he lies, he will be violating a genuine moral principle.

Similarly, Kant had strict opinions about what gives our actions moral merit. An action is not moral because of the consequences, but because of the purity of the intent and the reasons for which it is executed. Kant thought that the only reason that gives any action moral worth is if that action is done out of respect for the moral law alone. So, in the case of our employee considering skipping work to fish, if he goes to work simply because he fears getting behind, or fears the consequences should he be found out, his action would have no moral worth. He would be motivated by selfish reasons, and not motivated by the fact that it is the right thing to do *because he has a duty to go to work.* In the next section we will look at another important aspect Kant's moral theory, the connection between autonomy and dignity.

4.3 Kant and the Dignity of Persons

Kant believed that every rational being is endowed with **dignity**, and worthy of **respect**. Because of this he argued that no rule of conduct or moral maxim could be justified if following such rules and maxim violated our human dignity. We possess this dignity by virtue of the kind of being we are. We are **rational** and **free** beings, and Kant believed that this was what made us worthy of respect; therefore, we should honor each other's best interests and **autonomy**. He argued that the categorical imperative was roughly equivalent to another formula of the moral law that sets forth conditions as to how we should treat ourselves and other rational beings. Kant addresses what is often referred to as **the principle of dignity** in the following passage.

If then there is a supreme practical principle or, in respect of the human will, a categorical imperative, it must be one which, being drawn from the conception of that which is necessarily an end for everyone because it is an end in itself, constitutes an objective principle of will, and can therefore serve as a universal practical law. The foundation of this principle is: rational nature exists as an end in itself. Man necessarily conceives his own existence as being so; so far then this is a subjective principle of human actions. But every other rational being regards its existence similarly, just on the same rational principle that holds for me:[*] so that it is at the same time an objective principle, from which as a supreme practical law all laws of the will must be capable of being deduced. Accordingly the practical imperative will be as follows: **So act as to treat**

humanity, whether in thine own person or in that of any other, in every case as an end withal, never as means only. We will now inquire whether this can be practically carried out.[3]

___

Human beings are ends in themselves.   By this, Kant means that we each have intrinsic value that is not dependent on anyone else.   When we treat each other solely as a means to our own selfish ends, we are violating one another's dignity.   In other words, whenever we act, we must honor each other's best interests and never use others merely as *tools*, for our own purposes. The latter, amounts to "using people," and Kant recognized the inherent affront to our dignity that such treatment causes. We can readily see how this formula of the categorical imperative would apply to the case of our employee considering whether to skip work in order to fish. How would he be treating his boss and his fellow employees if he lies in order to escape work? He would be treating them merely as a means to his enjoyment, and using deception in order to hide that fact. This violates the principle of dignity, and so it would be immoral.   As we will see, many philosophers who do not accept Kant's theory believe that Kant, nonetheless, discovered something important in his analysis of human dignity, and they believe that the principle of dignity is an important feature of any reasonable moral perspective.   In the next section, we will look at two important criticisms of Kant's theory, and the attempt by contemporary philosopher, W.D. Ross to revise Kant's theory to remedy the problems that are raised by these criticisms.

4.4 The Noble Lie, Conflicting Rules, and W.D. Ross's Approach

The first major criticism of Kant's theory addresses his contention that it is never under any circumstances acceptable to tell a lie. However, it is fairly easy to think of examples in which one might need to tell a lie to save someone's life. Imagine that you have a Jewish neighbor who has been lately harassed by a local white supremacist group. She has been worried because she has received threats to herself and her children. One night after receiving a threat in the mail, she asks to hide in your house overnight, for she fears that they might try to break into her home that night and hurt her or her children. You agree to allow them to stay in your home. Sure enough, later that evening you hear a pounding on your door. You open it and are confronted by four menacing men dressed in neo-Nazi uniforms. The leader demands "Do you have any filthy Jews in your house?" What would you do? Many people would say that the stakes are so high, and that it is clear what the supremacists intend, so it would be permissible to not only deny them entry to your home, but to say "no," and perhaps attempt to mislead them to avert a serious crime. This kind of example poses what is sometimes called the "noble lie." Lying is usually considered wrong. But perhaps there are times when the ends do justify the means in certain special circumstances. The problem with Kant's approach is that it ignores all such circumstances and the consequences that would likely occur if our heroic neighbor tells the neo-Nazi's the truth. How can this be right? Kant defended his position by saying that in these kinds of cases, we can never be in fact certain about the consequences of telling the truth. However, if we lie, we can be logically certain that we have violated a moral law. Therefore, a rational person should act to avoid the evil that is *certain* if they disobey the moral rule, rather than act to avoid an evil that is only *possible*.

There are two problems that Kant's response ignores. First, Kant is certain that our heroic neighbors' "lie" could not meet the requirements of the categorical imperative. But if we lie under these circumstances, our maxim would not be that any time the going gets rough that we can lie to escape the possible consequences. It is not a case of universalizing the rightness of lying as a rule. Rather, we would only be willing to state that in *such specific circumstances* it is permissible to tell a lie.[4] Would not most, if not all, rational people allow such an exception in cases such as the neo-Nazi example?

The second problem with Kant's theory is that because he views every moral rule as absolutely binding at all times, we must by necessity find ourselves in impossible dilemmas whenever we are confronted with circumstances in which two rules conflict. Kant denied that such cases actually exist. However, again, it is relatively easy to generate such cases, and they do in fact occur. In fact, the case we just considered presents us with such a conflict of rules. Notice that when our heroic neighbor is asked to tell the leader whether she is hiding any Jews, she is not simply being presented with a choice between lying or not lying in which she will choose between obeying the moral rule not to lie, and choose to act on selfish motives. This situation is not like the case of the employee who calls in sick just so that he can go fishing with his friend. The heroic neighbor is also protecting her own life and the lives of other human beings. Her intent to do so is honorable, and the fact that she agreed to hide them gives her an obligation because there is now a trust between herself and her Jewish neighbors. We have two conflicting moral rules and thus, two conflicting duties; the duty to tell the truth, and the duty to protect the innocent who are now relying on her. If Kant is correct about moral rules, all are equally binding. Thus, in order to honor one rule, it would seem we must violate the other. This leaves us in an insoluble dilemma.

W.D. Ross, a twentieth century deontologist suggested that we could revise some aspects of Kant's theory, while maintaining the spirit of the approach. Ross believed that Kant was correct in thinking that moral laws are categorical and universal, but Ross denied that each and every moral rule could be obeyed equally in every situation. In some circumstances, like those we discussed in our previous example, we must make a decision between conflicting moral rules. Ross made a distinction between **prima facie moral duties**, and **actual moral duties.** The former involves cases that are straightforward, like the case of our employee lying to his boss in order to go fishing. We have prima facie duty not to lie, and barring any extraordinary cases in which we are confronted with a conflicting obligation, we should obey that rule. In such straightforward cases, our prima facie duty is our actual duty. However, in cases like the heroic neighbor when there are two conflicting prima facie duties and we cannot do both, we must rationally decide which duty is most **stringent**. By stringent, Ross means that one of the moral rules must take precedent in that particular circumstance. Thus, Ross would ask, would not all rational beings agree that our heroic neighbor has a more stringent duty to protect her neighbor and her children in *these narrow circumstances* that would outweigh telling a violent group of people who wish them ill, the truth? In such cases, the more stringent duty is our actual duty, so it is the one that should be performed.[5]

In concluding this chapter, we should consider whether Kant needed to maintain that we should ignore consequences altogether when making moral decisions. Perhaps there could be another way of approaching cases when two or more moral duties conflict with one another. We could agree with Kant that, in general, moral rules should be obeyed. At the same time, conflicts of rules do occur. In such cases, we could decide which duty is more stringent by weighing the moral consequences of following one rule over another. We may conclude that the duty that poses the most good, and best preserves the dignity of the most rational agents, is the more stringent duty. While this is not a solution that Kant would have accepted it may be a fruitful compromise between the deontological and rule utilitarian theories, that honors the concerns for impartiality and human dignity that both theories seek to promote.

So far in this book we have examined how ethical theories can apply to the workplace. Employees and managers alike are daily confronted with situations and decisions in which these theories come into play.

---

[1] Kant, Immanuel, *Fundamental Principles for the Metaphysic of Morals*, trans., Thomas Kingsmill Abbott, published online at eBooks@Adelaide, University of Adelaide Library, http://www.library.adelaide.edu.au/etext/k/k16prm/k16prm.zip, 2004.

[2] Ibid.

[3] Ibid.

[4] Anscombe, Elizabeth, "Modern Moral Philosophy," *Philosophy*, 33 (1958), p. 3.

[5] Ross, W.D. *The Right and the Good*, Oxford University Press, 1930, reprinted in Ethics: Selections from Classical and Contemporary Writers, 5th ed., Holt, Rinhart, and Winston.

CHAPTER FIVE: Claims about Moral and Legal Rights

It is nearly impossible to go through a day, without hearing or reading about someone demanding his/her rights. Contemporary Western societies have come to focus on the concept of rights more than any other moral concept.   In the United States, we have a "Bill of Rights," and our entire constitution lays the foundation for numerous legal rights.   However, the concept of rights has a complicated and widely debated history.   Moral and legal philosophers diverge in their views about what constitutes a right, as well as how rights are acquired and about how assertions about rights are justified.   Moreover, people commonly confuse moral and legal claims, and as a result often have a distorted understanding of their actual legal rights. Even worse, they sometimes do not make reasonable moral demands, simply because they assume they have no legal recourse.   For these reasons, when examining business ethics, it is important to briefly examine the development of the idea of a right and to clarify what is typically meant by moral rights and legal rights.

5.1 What is meant by a right?

What do we mean by a right?   In general, when we assert a **right** to something, we are making a claim with the corresponding expectation that our claim should in some way be honored by others on moral or legal grounds.   For example, if a person commits a felony by tampering with your personal mail, it is likely that you will claim that your right to privacy has been compromised.   If a person steals your car you may well claim that they have taken your property, thereby violating your property rights.   From these examples it is clear that we make claims about different types of things.   Our privacy is important to us, but so are our cars; however, clearly privacy and cars are different sorts of things.   Thus, we can say that when we make claims about rights, we are making claims about our interests broadly defined.   Some of these interests might be material, whereas others are less tangible but equally vital to us.

Contemporary theorists often make a distinction between positive rights and negative rights.   A **positive right** is a claim that you are moral or legally entitled to something, and this implies that one or more persons have an obligation to provide it.   For example, most people in the United States believe that equal access to public education is a positive right, and not a privilege.   And accordingly, there is a legal mandate to provide it in every state.   Likewise, if two people complete a monetary transaction over a piece of property as agreed, there is a moral and legal expectation that the buyer may take possession of the property.   In other words, the buyer has a right to that property.   A **negative right** is a claim that you are morally or legally entitled not to be treated in a certain fashion.   For this reason, negative rights sometimes are referred to as barrier rights, because they delineate a set of conditions about how people treat one another in various situations.[1]   The previous example of the complaint that your privacy had been violated when someone opened your mail is a case of asserting a negative right.   Most philosophers also agree that rights of both kinds involve corresponding duties or legal obligations. This means that if you possess a genuine right to something, then others who are party to your claim have a moral or legal obligation to satisfy it. However, what are our rights? On what grounds do we come to possess these rights?   Are there natural and unalienable rights? What is the difference between moral and legal rights, if any? These

66

questions, more than how we define what is meant by a right, have been the focus of centuries of philosophical debate.

5.2 Various Conceptions of Rights: A brief overview

The concept of a moral and legal right is a relatively modern concept in western history. The concept of a right began to form during the European Renaissance, and did not enter into formal moral and political doctrines until the 17th century. Prior to this time, the notion of a rightful claim seemed to be solely attached to the idea of certain privileges and powers that a person possessed or did not possess based on his/her social rank or position. Throughout the middle ages, the problem of judging rightful claims was understood by virtue of a person's role in the universal order of things as determined by clarifying the person's duties owed to lord, king, church or God. Thus, if a person were a serf, an Earl, or a kings' retainer, he/she would have various duties but also privileges associated with a rank and role. Such claims to certain privileges were not absolute or in any manner inalienable, rather they were thought to be legitimate, but dependent on a person maintaining rank and favor. In the seventeenth and eighteen centuries, such notions gave way to other legal concepts such as an "Englishman's birthright," and more abstractly, the notion of **natural rights**.[2] It is this latter notion that has had tremendous influence in modern Anglo-American political philosophy. This notion of a right is what we find in the United States Declaration of Independence. Such rights are said to be inalienable, meaning that they cannot be taken from someone due to a change in status, and are said to be natural, in that they are possessed at birth. Merely in virtue of being human a person has certain legitimate claims upon others. Having these rights honored is not subject to the preferences or feelings of others, or upon personal merit. Since the seventeenth century, philosophers have debated about the basis and content of alleged natural rights. Are natural rights somehow the most basic of our moral concepts? Do the other concepts of virtues and rules that we formulate stem from these rights? Or, as many assert today, are claims about rights only meaningful in the context of particular religious or secular moral theories? Why would rights stem from our notions of virtue or moral rules? Consider the following. Anyone can make a moral or legal claim to something and demand it because it is a "right." However, a person can clearly be in error about such claims. In fact such claims can be made without the person having any power or reasonable expectation of the claim being honored. For example, a person could assert the right to be recognized as the "King of Venus," and demand that the United Nations recognize his/her sovereignty over that planet. No rational person would take such a claim seriously. Moreover, what would count as possessing the basis for this right? If claims about rights can be sometimes reasonable and legitimate, but sometimes not reasonable or legitimate, what criteria do we use to determine when such claims are valid? If we assume that it is another right, then we can in turn demand the basis of that right. This is the crux of much of the debate over the basis of rights, and many philosophers now think that claims about rights must be justified by an argument that invariably involves one or more moral theories.

5.3 Moral and Legal Rights

To say that someone has a **moral right**, means that the person morally deserves the object of the claim, regardless of whether it is a positive or negative claim. However, possessing such rights does not guarantee that others will acknowledge or honor them. Moreover, there are some moral rights that do not seem to merit legal recognition. For example, we might reasonably expect a good friend to help us out, especially if we have helped them many times before. We might say that in this sense, we have a moral right to their help. However, this would not imply that we necessarily had a legal claim to their help, such that they had a legal obligation to help us. As discussed in the first chapter, there is an overlap between ethics and law, but they are not identical. **Legal rights** are a specific subset of rights. To say that a person has a legal right means that he/she has a claim that is recognized under the law. This typically means that if we fail to observe that right, then the person has legal recourse under the law to due process, including seeking penalties and damages against us or the state. It should likewise be clear, that failure to recognize a person's reasonable claim does not show that they do not have moral grounds for that claim. In fact, it may be that the claim should be recognized. On other hand, sometimes individuals and communities invoke legal rights that to many, are morally questionable. For example, in the United States the practice of seizing property by "immanent domain" is the subject of such a controversy.

Another subset of rights is referred to as **special rights**. These are rights that are based on customs that do not involve a clear moral or legal basis. For example, some types of employee privileges in the work place might be classified in this fashion, such as employee-only gyms or dining rooms. Thus, someone may have a "right" to such facilities, but only by virtue of being an employee at that company. Similar customary rights are recognized in private organizations and clubs. Often rights of this type do not involve any hard and fast rules, but are simply understood.   In other words, these "rights" are better classified as privileges   A warning about special rights in the workplace should be noted.   If an employer permits or denies a staff member the right to a workplace privilege without reason, it is possible that the employer is being unfair, and in some circumstances, may be guilty of violating anti-discrimination laws.

Some legal philosophers find it useful to distinguish between various kinds of legal rights.   In addition to the distinction between positive and negative rights, we can further classify rights by noting the different purposes that respecting these rights are aiming to fulfill. For example, certain types of positive rights are referred to as **welfare rights**.   These are rights that need to be respected in order for a person to have the capacity of a more basic right.   If we believe that people should have equal opportunities in the work place to compete for jobs, then it seems to be derivative that they have a right to the training as well as fair hiring practices that would make enjoying equal opportunity possible.   More controversially, many claim that universal health care is a moral right that should be mandated, meaning, made a legal right.   On this view, universal health care is seen as a basic welfare right.

In addition, some philosophers speak of **barrier rights** as a subset of negative rights. The right to privacy, the right to be protected from harassment, assault, and undue search and seizure are all examples of barrier rights. Such rights help define what is understood as necessary to respect regarding each individual's space, property, and person.

5.4 Competing Rights: Prima facie vs. Absolute Rights

Regardless of the various positions philosophers have taken about the nature of rights, there is clear agreement about that fact that different people's rights come into conflict. Balancing these rights constitutes one of the key responsibilities of government and the courts. If rights, like moral principles, can conflict then how can they be considered absolute? Does possessing an inalienable right guarantee that it will be honored all of the time, or in the way that a person may wish it to be honored at a particular time?   A person may have the right to free speech, which is a guaranteed constitutional right in the United States, but this fact does not license a person to go into a crowed public building and scream "fire" at the top of his/her lungs. This is a felony in many states of the union, and the person could be accused of inciting a riot thereby endangering public safety. In short, it would seem that the force of rights may be more like W.D. Ross's notion of a "prima facie moral duty."   In most cases such rights are to be honored, but when they conflict with the rights of others, then we must have a standard to decide in those circumstances, which stakeholder's rights are most stringent.   Clearly, it would therefore require appeal to a moral theory in order to justify which person's right should be honored at a particular time.   This provides us with another reason why the study of moral theories is indispensable in moral decision making.   We cannot rely on a doctrine of rights alone, in order to make all of our moral and legal decisions.

---

[1] Beauchamp, Tom, Bowie, Norman, Ethical Theory and Business, 2nd ed., Prentice Hall, 1983, p. 47.

[2] Benn, Stanley, Entry of Rights, *The Encyclopedia of Philosophy*, Volumes 7 and 8, Macmillan and Free Press, New York, 1967, p. 195.

CONCLUSION

After exploring several of the most influential moral theories informing contemporary moral debates, we discovered that business ethics is only one area of concern in a much larger matrix of moral issues that we confront daily in our society. As the current trend toward global capitalism continues to expand, there will be an increase both in the number of moral conflicts confronting businesses, as well as the complexity of these issues. The theories and applications explored in this text can help us address the current and future challenges confronting business, but only if we soberly and honestly examine our own character and conduct, both in respect to our overall life decisions and our business practices. We must also be prepared to face the hard questions about our institutions. While growing economies create wealth and the means of sustenance, they also create moral dilemmas that require is to ask ourselves "what are best ethical solutions"?

It is beyond the scope of this text either to fully endorse or fully critique any of the moral theories that we examined. The merits and demerits of each theory have been hotly debated by philosophers for centuries, and we have only explored some of these debates in this text. Nonetheless, studying these theories offers us a great deal of insight into what leading an ethical life in all respects involves. I will conclude this text with a few insights that I hope students of business, for whom this text has been largely written, might take to heart.

Character and Conduct: An Adequate Moral Perspective

One of the points that our examination of the theories of Kant and Mill revealed was that each in their own way began with the same metaphysical assumption about conduct. Both thought that being moral was primarily a matter of right action. However, both Kant and Mill championed opposing claims in this regard: Kant asserting that only principles and the proper will behind the conduct give it moral value and Mill asserting that only the consequences of actions matter in assessing the moral value of conduct. In both theories, we see a break with the classical perspective we examined in the second chapter of the text. However, I suggest that we can learn a great deal from Aristotle and Aquinas. In particular, we need to ask ourselves whether we can dispense with our concern for good character in our moral reasoning. Morality is about the kind of person that we strive to be, not merely behaving in a politically correct manner. For Aristotle, both moral rules and the nature of our desires, as well as our intentions matter in moral reasoning. Moreover, Aristotle recognized that we must sometimes consider the consequences of our actions in order to do the right thing. The kind of person that we become includes our moral character, which is a central part of our identity. Thus, if we are inconsistent in the various areas of our lives with our various relationships, it says a great deal about who we are. If I treat someone in my business dealings differently than I would a family member or a friend, am I acting with integrity? For example, if my family and friends deserve my honesty, then how can I defend being a dishonest worker?

With these things in mind, I suggest that people planning to enter business, either as employees or business owners in their own right, keep the following questions before themselves every working day.   What kind of person do I wish to be?   In my business activities, do I serve the interests of others as well as my own, or do I merely serve my own interests and create burdens in the lives of others?   Is the way that I operate at work a reflection of how I operate at home?   If not, how do I need to change?

It is only by asking ourselves such questions and committing ourselves to the task of displaying moral integrity in all aspects of our lives that we can begin to understand what it means to be a good person in business.   This ultimately is the goal of business ethics.